May 23, 2009

Mary,

I hope this book will transport you to a faraway place, at least for a little while.

And I hope you will have some tea while reading this.

Barbara

P.S. found this book at "FLOATING ISLAND"

Looking Deeply into Tea

Thoughts and Prayers

Looking Deeply into Tea
Thoughts and Prayers

Text by Shelley Richardson
Photographs by Bruce Richardson

Benjamin Press
205 East Fourth Street
Perryville, KY 40468

Other Books by Bruce & Shelley Richardson
A Year of Teas at the Elmwood Inn
A Tea for All Seasons
The Tea Table
The Great Tea Rooms of Britain
The Great Tea Rooms of America
The New Tea Companion
Tea in the City: New York

Copyright 2005
by Bruce & Shelley Richardson

Printed in China

Benjamin Press
205 East Fourth Street
Perryville, Kentucky 40468 USA
(800) 765-2139
www.elmwoodinn.com

ISBN 0-9663478-4-6

Teaism

To one who drinks from the true cup of teaism,
this book is dedicated to our dear friend and colleague,
Mary Freear Williams

Contents

Acknowledgements

We would like to express our deep gratitude to those who have
helped, inspired, and supported us in this project:

The Specialty Tea Institute, Joe Simrany, president;
The Tea Board of India;
The Tea Board of Sri Lanka;
Our editor at Benjamin Press, Mary Freear Williams;
Our photo editor, Ben Richardson;
Our staff, Jane Lanham, Masha Popkhadze, Jan Sheffield, and Amy Wise;
Our friend, Irene Humelsine;
and the people of India and Sri Lanka who work to
bring us our cup of tea.

Hymn to the Earth

Earth, in which lie the sea, the river and the other waters,
in which food and tea gardens come to be,
in which lives all that breathes and moves,
may she confer on us the finest of her yield.
Earth, in which the waters, common to all,
moving on all sides, flow unfailingly, day and night,
may she pour on us tea from many containers, and endow us with lustre.
May those born of thee, O Earth,
be for our welfare, free from sickness and waste,
wakeful through a long life, we shall become
bearers of tribute to thee.
Earth my mother, set me securely with bliss in full
accord with heaven,
O wise one,
uphold me in grace and splendor.

Based on *The Atharva-Veda*

Introduction

"Rise up nimbly and go on your Strange Journey
To the oceans of meanings"
Rumi

These words of Rumi's speak to my heart in the most profound way. I believe that each of us has a purpose here on this earth or, as Soren Kierkegaard put it, "sealed orders." We spend our lives searching for those orders. We travel down paths that ultimately lead us back into the place we know so well.

The truth is that we are the containers and the orders are already within us, close at hand every minute of every day. When we surrender to the One who holds the container, we begin discovering the orders and the magnificent journey of our lives at that very moment. The containers that we are become openings, great and holy temples full of spaciousness and beauty. Without any effort, everything becomes a sign and a gift showing us how to live with knowledge, purpose, and dignity.

When my husband journeyed to India and Sri Lanka in search of tea, he returned with many treasures. I remember passionately awaiting his return at the airport. Upon seeing him walking toward me after stepping off the plane, I realized that he was transparent. I could see through him as if he was a watery vapor floating in the air. I felt that if I touched him, he might evaporate before me. At that moment, I knew that what he had seen and felt in India had cracked open the container of his heart. For several days afterwards, we could only look deeply into each other's eyes because words could not be used. Later, when I saw the photographs he had taken of the beautiful tea workers and the natural beauty that surrounds the world of tea, I understood.

This book has grown out of our collaboration in work as well as in marriage. The photographs were an inspiration to me at once, and drew my heart into a place of worship as well as a place of communion with my husband. The meditations I have written were inspired by each photograph. I have kept them simple because I believe that is the way it should be.

Simplicity speaks to the heart, clears the mind, and reminds us of our origin. I think that the real life force that runs beneath what appears to be the surface is evident in these photographs. I have considered it a privilege to work with them.

Shelley Richardson

Looking Deeply into Tea
Thoughts and Prayers

My Teacher

When we learn about our nature
from what is given to us at birth,
and trust what is meant to be
by doing what is natural,
then we become buddhas and
teachers to each other,
glowing with an aura of life,
joy, and compassion.

Dancer

If you want to dance,
dance your truth.
Let the inner become the outer.
When you do,
the whole world will watch.

Sweet Fragrance

What sweet fragrance do you hold today?
It flows from earth to body, to fingertips,
to the tea leaf.
Knowing how to move within that is to live,
knowing all is one and the same.

Pure Heart

If we have no fear
the world will become a safe place.

Then, there will be no need for weapons.

Walking the Path

I would like to think
I could walk a path of serenity
not worrying if I did enough
this day or that,
each foot leaving a soft glimmer of light
upon the brown earth.
No need to be concerned with
what was before or after,
only what is here,
now,
calling.

Easy Traveling

Weary,
breathless,
trying to be several selves at once.
Surrender all to the divine Center.
Become busy carrying a full load
without burden.
Poised, and at peace.
No struggle.
No strain.
Easy traveling.

Path to Eternity

Eternity is the present moment.
Simplicity.
Beauty.
Bare feet touching earth
in harmony with nature
and each other.

Double Blossom

Dripping with the holy dew of baptism,
the soul bursts forth from its bud
cupping its delicate fragrance and
surrendering it into the world,
as if to say from a golden throat,
"Lose yourself and be found."

Boy with Hat

What mystery lies behind your eyes,
behind your luxurious face?
Your outer presence is a clue
to your inner presence.

In India the greeting is "Namaste."
I bow to the divine in you.

Do we bow together?
Do you see what is like you in me?
Do I see what is like me in you?

When we see that, we become one.

The Most Beautiful Temple

We travel all around the world
to the greatest temples
searching for miracles.
If only we could remember
that we have what we are longing for
within our own bodies,
our most beautiful temples.

Faces

No need for words.
Your faces speak
an eloquent language
from the soul.

Centered

When we are centered in love,
beauty,
compassion,
and kindness,
our burdens may look heavy
but they are not.
They are easy to carry, and
we are surrounded by radiant light.

Tea Garden

In this world
it is easy to travel
to new places and fascinating landscapes.
What matters is
that we lift the veil from our eyes,
open ourselves to a new voyage of perception,
and arrive in paradise.

New Creation

Ah, but to be a butterfly upon a tea leaf,
to decipher the hieroglyphics upon a wing,
or trust the darkness of transformation.

I bow to the god before me,
and drink the essence of
beauty's sweet nectar.

Bells

I once heard the bells at Chartres Cathedral ringing,
calling me to my true home.
There, I discovered a key
that unlocked a myriad of other bells.
Muslim,
Hindu,
Buddhist,
Jewish,
Christian,
each ringing a different sound
but calling to the same place.

Nirvana

"The unborn, the undying,"
that's what the Buddha said.
"Here earth, air, water and fire do not arise."
Follow the path that leads to this realization
and we will find our true nature.

Balance

Balance is peace.
It is the present moment.
No dwelling in the past or gazing at the future.

Tea in the teacup,
just the right amount,
makes the perfect cup.

Cupping

I looked at the ancient tea bowl
behind glass in the museum.

Its beauty and simplicity beckoned to me.

My gaze brought it into my heart.
It became my soul for that moment.

I turned it on its side
and felt a pouring out.

I turned it back
and felt a filling up.

Suffering Servant

It is only through suffering,
eroding away the hardness around the heart,
that we become the bodichitta.

The rivers of forgiveness and understanding
carve the way out of the deep
canyons of the soul,
becoming bridges that
reveal the pure radiant light of Love.

Being There

My presence
is the greatest gift
I am able to offer to you.
In my unique way
I will help you.
I will work with you.
I will give my very life for you.
If you are suffering,
I will give you loving kindness,
understanding, and compassion.

Offering

This work I do is an offering
from my hand and heart.
Let imagination awaken the power
that is within each leaf,
releasing healing communion
throughout the world.

Shakti

In late morning
I feel the touch of
the Divine Mother.
Her warmth and radiance
surround and enter my body.
My hand touches Hers
as I pick the tea leaves.
She is in me as I am in Her.
As I work today,
let Her face be mine.

Invitation

We are the ones who challenge God
to reveal a face.
We are the ones who often miss
the divine moments of life
because we look in the wrong places.

We find our greatest teachers in
the eyes of the humble.

Monet's Tea Picker

Surrounded by a halo of light,
you become Camille.
"To tremble at the shock of colors,"
your beauty becomes brushstrokes upon my memory.

My Gift

May you be kissed
by the warm spirit of compassion,
embraced by quiet protecting arms
of peace.

May the life giving energy
of the Universe surge through your veins
like a wild river,
opening your heart to the creative power of
Love.

64

Contemplation

Silence
like a sheltering canopy,
protects and holds us inside a wordless place.

Within this stillness,
the breath of Eternity gives way to awe.

Ganga

Powerful,
like a river goddess,
Ganga,
falling from the Milky Way,
cascading thru Shiva's curls.
Her power is to forgive and purify,
to wash one clean in the Ganges.

Garuda

Let suffering come.
Let it be felt,
but let it arise as if it were
the great Garuda
in its flight across the sky.
It has left no trace as
the clearing comes.

Going Home

Take a step toward home.
It is always the most
simple
and
direct path.
Let the questions
fall away.
The answers don't matter.
Just carry what you are given
and start walking.

Black Madonna

To be covered by God's shadow is holy.

May we walk through
Your portals into the unseen world.

Birth us with invisible light.
Suckle us with earthy, fiery energy.
Nurture us with child-like eyes.

And, by your glory and fierce embrace,
illumine us
with love,
with truth,
with grace.

Great Mother

In the picking of tea,
I think about the manifestation of the Mother.
She is everything.
She comes without fail,
watching over her children.
She is the Wise One.
Her power flows as she picks
the delicate bud.
She wears a golden halo around her head
and carries the basket of tea
as it it were sweet compassion,
ready to pour out onto the world.

Wise One

The Great Mother is everywhere.
She comes down from the mountain
on the breath of the wind.
She is the Wise One, the Grandmother.
She comes to lead us back into the Cosmic Womb.
Take Her hand and begin the journey.
Her secret surrounds Her like soft billowy clouds.
Arising from the mist, wisdom whispers,
"Death is Life and Life is Eternal."

Credits

Page 5   Excerpted from *The Book of Tea* by Okakura Kakuzo. Published and copyright by the Charles E. Tuttle Company, Inc., 1956.

Page 59 With thanks to *Monet* by Jude Welton. Published by Dorling Kindersley. Copyright by Dorling Kindersley Limited, 1992.

About the Photographs

I have had the good fortune to see much of the world through the lens of a camera. Beginning in elementary school with my Kodak Brownie, my life's experiences have been captured forever on film, and now, in digital files.

As a photographer, I have the good fortune of remembering much of what I have seen because I can relive my adventures over and over by viewing the slides and photographs I have compiled. I sometimes wonder how non-photographers remember their lives without the aid of a camera. Are the images they collect in their minds as vivid as the ones I relive on film?

I have never been in such photo-rich environments as those I found in India and Sri Lanka. I felt like a hunter with my camera poised to shoot whenever an image stirred to life before me. It might be the colorful flash of a woman's scarf as she walked through a monotone dessert, or a ray of light reflected off the bud of a tea plant as the mist lifted.

Often my attention was drawn to the faces of the tea workers I met. Their deep eyes and cocoa faces drew me into their world. Their innocence was captivating. Their smiles were ever present.

My aim is never to simply shoot a "pretty picture." I am successful when people see my photographs and hearts are moved. My soul was touched when I encountered these tea workers and the lands where they live. My hope is that you will feel the same emotions I felt. I will be pleased if, when you drink a cup of tea, you look deeply into the cup, see the women who picked your tea, and pause to honor them before you drink.

Bruce Richardson

Photography Notes

Page 14.   I photographed this tea picker on the Pussimbing Tea Estate in Darjeeling, India. A plastic cloth wraps her like an apron to protect her clothing from being torn as she weaves her way through the waist-high tea bushes.

Page 16.   This young girl danced for American guests on the Puttabong Estate in Darjeeling. Tea workers and their families crowded around the pavilion to see the spectacle. Her fluid motion and the graceful movement of her hands were mesmerizing for both guests and residents.

Page 18.   I met this woman on the steep, winding dirt road that leads to the Tum Song Tea Estate in Darjeeling. She had waited patiently that afternoon to greet us as we slowly made our way to her village.

Page 20.   The faces of the children of Darjeeling are welcoming in their innocence and purity. Families on tea plantations are generally of Nepalese descent.

Page 22.   I met this proud woman at sunrise as she walked along one of the stone roads on the Ambootia Tea Estate in Darjeeling. She was on her way to work in the offices of the tea factory.

Page 24.   I saw this man pedaling his load of rags on the street in New Delhi. It was my first day in India and I was amazed at the ease on his face as he wheeled his gargantuan load along the bustling highway.

Page 26.   This is one of the most serendipitous photos I have taken. I quickly shot this scene through the open window of my vehicle as I left the Sonapur Tea Estate in Assam. These three women with their freshly picked tea are heading to the weighing station at the end of their workday.

Page 28.   The sight of a tea blossom is a rare thing on a tea plantation. The women pick the unopened tea bud and the first two leaves for the best tea. I found this plant in bloom in an abandoned Sri Lankan field.

Page 30.   This young son of a tea worker was standing on the front porch of his school on the Puttabong Tea Estate in Darjeeling. Each tea estate has its own school.

Photography Notes

Page 32.   Nothing can prepare you for your first glimpse of the Taj Mahal. The scene before me was enhanced by the colorful clothing of this Hindu tourist.

Page 34.   This man's smiling face beckoned me as I scanned a crowd that stood along a Darjeeling roadside. His rugged complexion, etched by years of working on the sunny slopes of the Himalayan foothills, spoke volumes about his life's history.

Page 36.   Nearly everything on a tea estate is recycled – including the grass clippings. I encountered a young man bearing this tremendous load up a Darjeeling mountain road. He passed me without any indication of weariness.

Page 38.   My first night in a tea garden was spent in a bungalow just down the road from this lakeside vista in the Sri Lankan highlands. Eucalyptus trees shade the manicured tea bushes from the hot equatorial sun.

Page 40.   I photographed this butterfly on a tea bush for Shelley. Her love of butterflies is matched only by her affinity for beautiful teas.

Page 42.   This mass of bells lines the walls of the Kamakshya temple near Guwahati in Assam. Pilgrims from around the world come here to pray for fertility.

Page 44.   One of my favorite holy sites in Sri Lanka is the Buddhist temple in the former capitol of Kandy. In this picture, a group of young Buddhist women approach the entrance as the late afternoon sun illuminates their robes with its waning rays.

Page 46.   The tea taster for the Tata Tea Company in Calcutta will sip and spit over 400 teas each day. Three busy men weigh precise measurements of tea before brewing the liquor for endless rows of tasting cups that will be rolled to his waiting lips.

Page 48.   The heart of any tea brokerage is the cupping room. This photograph was taken in the second largest cupping room in the world, located in Guwahati, Assam.

Page 50.   The Hugli River flows peacefully through the chaos of Calcutta. Using a telephoto lens, I was able to catch this man in a contemplative moment as he gazed at the passing traffic.

Photography Notes

Page 52.   This vibrant elderly man approached me in the town plaza of Darjeeling. He proudly showed me the gigantic brass belt buckle that was given to him on the occasion of his retirement as manager of one of the tea estates.

Page 54.   This smiling tea picker, with her woven sun hat, greeted me from a tea field in the lowlands of Assam.

Page 56.   I met this woman on the Puttabong Tea Estate in Darjeeling, and asked if I could photograph her. She agreed, and before long she had invited me to see the inside of her simple home.

Page 58.   Many tea pickers carry umbrellas to protect them from the harsh sun. They present a whimsical flash of color in an unending field of green.

 Page 60. Most tea pickers are women. They are usually in the fields as the sun comes up in order to finish before the hot midday temperatures. This picture was taken at the Kirkoswold Tea Estate in Sri Lanka.

Page 62.   Using a 300mm lens, I was able to capture the contemplative mood of this Darjeeling tea picker as she stood in the middle of an endless tea garden.

Page 64.   Abundant water is needed to grow tea. The moisture-laden trade winds of the Indian Ocean shed their rain as they flow over the highest mountains of Sri Lanka. The water races in cascading torrents as it snakes it way from 8000 feet to sea level.

Page 66.   I woke up with the rising sun after a humid night in a Sri Lankan tea garden. A beautiful lake vista greeted me as I opened the back door to my bungalow. Row upon row of tea plants covered the hills in every direction.

Page 68.   I captured the image of these two Tamil women making their way home from the tea fields. They pick between 35 and 60 kilos of tea leaves each day before the hot Sri Lankan sun drives them from the fields.

Photography Notes

Page 70.   I shot a series of nearly 25 photographs of this young woman and her baby as they watched the festivities at a greeting ceremony on a Darjeeling tea estate. They were enraptured by the music and dancing in front of them, as if nothing else existed in the world.

Page 72.   Mothers and daughters often work side by side in the tea fields of Darjeeling. These women told me they prefer to work in the fields rather than the tea factories because the men are not there to listen to their conversations.

Page 74.   I met this elderly woman sitting on a Darjeeling hillside. She had lived on the tea estate all her life and was now nearly blind. Behind her lay the ancient hills of Sikkim. Her aged face seemed nearly as wise as the mountainous setting that framed her.

About the Author and Photographer

Shelley Richardson published her first book of recipes from the historic Elmwood Inn, *A Year of Teas at the Elmwood Inn*, in 1994. That book was quickly followed by *A Tea for All Seasons* in 1996, and *The Tea Table* in 2003. Tea rooms across the country regularly turn to her books of tea recipes for inspiration. Shelley is co-owner of Elmwood Inn Fine Teas, an accomplished clarinetist, and travels the world in search of labyrinths.

Bruce Richardson's photographs have appeared in six previous books from Benjamin Press as well as the magazines *Fresh Cup*, *Tea Time* and *TEA*. He is the tea blender and co-owner of Elmwood Inn Fine Teas. He holds two degrees in choral conducting and was a professional musician before entering the world of tea.